Search and Rescue Dogs

Dog Tales:
True Stories About Amazing Dogs

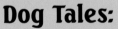

Search and Rescue Dogs

Marie-Therese Miller

CHELSEA CLUBHOUSE

An Imprint of Chelsea House Publishers

Search and Rescue Dogs
© 2007 by Infobase Publishing

J 636.7 Miller

All rights reserved. No part of this book may be reproduced or
utilized in any form or by any means, electronic or mechanical,
including photocopying, recording, or by any information storage or
retrieval systems, without permission in writing from the publisher. For
information contact:

Chelsea Clubhouse
An imprint of Infobase Publishing
132 West 31st Street
New York, NY 10001

ISBN-10: 7910-9037-X
ISBN-13: 978-0-7910-9037-4

Library of Congress Cataloging-in-Publication Data
Miller, Marie-Therese.
    Search and Rescue dogs / Marie-Therese Miller.
        p. cm. — (Dog tales, true stories about amazing dogs)
    Includes bibliographical references and index.
    ISBN 0-7910-9037-X (hardcover)
    1. Search dogs—United States—Juvenile literature. 2. Rescue dogs—
United States—Juvenile literature. I. Title. II. Series.
SF428.73.M55 2007
636.7'0886—dc22   2006024086

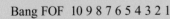

Chelsea House and Chelsea Clubhouse books are available at special
discounts when purchased in bulk quantities for businesses, associations,
institutions, or sales promotions. Please call our Special Sales Department
in New York at (212) 967-8800 or (800) 322-8755.

You can find Chelsea House and Chelsea Clubhouse on the
World Wide Web at http://www.chelseahouse.com

Development Editor: Anna Prokos
Text Design: Annie O'Donnell
Cover Design: Ben Peterson

Printed in the United States of America

Bang FOF 10 9 8 7 6 5 4 3 2 1

This book is printed on acid-free paper.

All links and Web addresses were checked and verified to be correct at
the time of publication. Because of the dynamic nature of the Web, some
addresses and links may have changed since publication and may no
longer be valid.

Contents

1

Team to the Rescue

Jake carefully made his way across still-warm steel beams. The unleashed dog treaded carefully through the smoldering rubble and treaded lightly on the thick layer of ash that blanketed the ground. With her gas mask on, Mary Flood commanded her dog to seek. The pair worked for days with other search and rescue teams. These specialized teams were hoping to find survivors buried beneath the collapsed buildings of the World Trade Center site after terrorists attacked the two skyscrapers on September 11, 2001.

1

Mary Flood and her search and rescue dog, Jake, work together to help locate people who have been caught in a disaster.

Tragically, there were few buried survivors. Jake alerted his handler to dead bodies with a silent downward tip of his nose.

Jake has been specifically trained to work at disaster sites like this one. His human handler, Mary Flood of Bountiful, Utah, began training the black Labrador retriever after she adopted the pup through an animal rescue organization. Flood learned the day after she adopted Jake that he had a twice-broken leg and a displaced hip. She had fallen in love with her "big beautiful black Lab," so Flood dug deep into her bank account to restore Jake to health. Jake underwent a costly leg operation and eight months of healing time. Flood had saved Jake's life. Now, he would help her save the lives of others.

Flood started training Jake to be a search and rescue dog for Utah Task Force One of the Federal Emergency Management Agency (FEMA). Utah Task Force One is part of a national network of 28 search and rescue teams managed by FEMA. Firefighters, doctors, nurses, and other volunteer specialists—including search and rescue dogs and their handlers—all play a role in the Task Force's work. Search and rescue dogs are taught to locate lost people following a natural disaster, such as an **avalanche** or earthquake, or after a human-made disaster, such as a bombing. The dogs can also be trained to find missing persons in the wilderness.

DOG IN TRAINING

To ready Jake for search and rescue work, Flood taught him obedience. She started with simple commands, like "stay" and "come." She took him to different places to practice his obedience skills. He needed to understand that "sit" meant the same thing in the kitchen as it did on the wooded trail. Jake worked hard at mastering these skills. He became so obedient that Flood was able to unleash him in a crowded area, have him walk 75 feet ahead of her, and command him to "sit stay."

It is vital for search and rescue dogs to listen to their handlers and obey commands immediately. Rescue work can be dangerous to the dogs and their handlers, so following orders is critical. At one site, Jake was searching when a large dump truck began to unload, putting the dog directly in harm's way. Jake's ability to react to his handler's commands removed him from a life-threatening position.

Search and rescue dogs use their amazing sense of smell to locate individuals. A person sheds approximately 40,000 dead skin cells, called **rafts**, every minute. These rafts have a particular odor that a canine can detect and follow as they float on air currents. This is known as **air scenting**.

Flood began training Jake to use air scenting for wilderness searches. A helper held Jake as Flood walked a short distance away and ducked behind a low shrub. The helper released Jake so he could find Flood. When Jake located her, he was rewarded with lots of praise and some food. Over time, this simple

KEEPING JAKE HEALTHY

Mary Flood's top job as a search and rescue canine handler is to make sure that her dog, Jake, stays well. That's why she feeds him a nutritious diet, which does not include any sugar. Before he works, she gives the command "take water," so that Jake will drink and be well hydrated for the task at hand.

Each of Flood's and Jake's grueling twelve-hour night shifts at the World Trade Center disaster site ended with a visit to the Veterinary Medical Assistance Teams. The veterinarians there checked Jake for dehydration and examined his paws, eyes, and ears for injury. Then, they gave him a warm bath to remove the muck from his fur. Sometimes, Flood and Jake would visit a chiropractor who would ease their sore muscles with a well-deserved massage.

More than five years after the terrorist attacks, canine medical experts continue to study Jake's health. They want to be certain that he suffered no ill effects from his exposure to the ash and fumes at the disaster site. Jake undergoes plenty of veterinary check-ups, which include Magnetic Resonance Imaging (MRI) of his nasal cavities.

Jake's health is a clue to the health of humans who worked at the World Trade Center site after the terrorist attacks. If the veterinarians detect any long-term health problems in the dog, they will know what to be on the lookout for in humans who worked there. Jake continues to receive a clean bill of health. In fact, he hasn't stopped working. Jake still participates in search and rescue missions when he is needed.

game of hide and seek progressed to more rugged terrain and on longer trails.

With plenty of practice finds under his belt, Jake moved on to tougher searches. The next step was to locate a hidden stranger. This taught Jake to air scent for another person's smell, not just his handler's. After Jake found the hidden individual, he was taught to complete a find/refind. This means that Jake would race back to Flood and lead her to the person he had discovered.

This dedicated training prepared Jake and Flood for the time they were called to find an older man who was lost in a canyon in Arizona. The man had lost his footing and fallen 70 feet. For five days, the lost man endured grueling heat and frigid nights until a search and rescue team found him. Jake and Mary Flood were part of that successful team. Experts told the searchers that the man probably would have died if he'd spent one more day in the canyon.

RESPONDING TO DISASTER

Jake and Flood enjoy helping out with search and rescue during disaster work. To operate safely and efficiently at a disaster site, Jake had to learn to respond to his handler's directional commands. Flood practiced directional commands with Jake on an area shaped like a baseball diamond. The diamond had wooden pallets positioned at each base. This taught Jake to climb upon objects when Flood said, "hup." Flood stood at home base and directed Jake from base to base with the commands: "left," "right," "go out," "go back," or "stay." In addition to verbal commands, she used hand signals to direct Jake. Disaster sites are noisy places, filled with whirring helicopters and roaring truck engines. Sometimes it can be hard for dogs to hear their handler's verbal commands, so it's important for the dogs to understand specific hand signals.

During his training, Jake was taught to give a 30-second bark when he found a buried person alive. To teach Jake this skill, a volunteer hid in a rubber barrel, called a bark barrel or alert hole. If Jake gave the proper bark upon locating the person, Flood rewarded him with a dog treat.

Disaster areas are filled with unstable rubble, so Jake learned to be sure-footed while searching. To practice **agility**, Flood had Jake climb ladders and crawl through tunnels. He crossed wobbly chain link bridges and balanced on wooden planks.

For more true-to-life training, Jake practices on Utah Task Force One's rubble pile. There, he can work on the types of debris found at a disaster site, such as crushed glass on rock or splintered wood. A volunteer sometimes hides beneath the rubble so that Jake can locate the person. This type of practice training is vital for disaster searches, such as the search at the World Trade Center.

Disaster work can be terribly sad when no people are found alive. Still, Flood knows that Jake's amazing scenting skills help bring closure to families of disaster victims.

2 Wilderness Search and Rescue

If a child has wandered away from her home or if disoriented hikers become lost in the woods in Illinois, Sherri Gallagher will receive an urgent phone call. Gallagher and Lektor, her 5-year-old German shepherd, immediately respond, day or night, to find a missing person in an Illinois cornfield or thickly forested location.

Gallagher is a member of the Chicago Regional Search and Rescue, which is a chapter of the American Rescue Dog Association. This national group

Lektor poses with his handler, Sherri Gallagher. Lektor and Gallagher immediately respond to a call to search for a missing person.

promotes the use of German shepherds for search and rescue missions. Lektor is specially trained in wilderness search and rescue. The first step in becoming a wilderness search and rescue team, like Gallagher and Lektor, is for the handler to choose a puppy with search and rescue potential.

When seeking good search and rescue pups, Gallagher looks for a breeder who is known for producing healthy and reliable working dogs. She finds breeders who only breed German shepherds that are successful in the sport of **Schutzhund**. *Schutzhund* is a German word that means protection dog. Dogs that participate in Schutzhund demonstrate obedience, tracking, and protection skills. If a puppy's mother and father did well in Schutzhund, the puppy has a good chance of inheriting useful working-dog genes, such as agility and scenting abilities.

Gallagher also tests the puppy's **temperament** to find potential search and rescue dogs. She looks for a puppy that loves to play because play is used in search and rescue dog training as a reward and to interest the canine in searching. To evaluate the pup's play drive, Gallagher crumples a piece of paper into a ball and throws it. She wants to see if the puppy will run after the paper ball to pick it up.

During her evaluation, Gallagher bangs a cooking pan near the puppy. She wants a pup that won't be frightened by the noise, but will trot over to

GERMAN SHEPHERD KNOW–HOW

German shepherds, Labrador and golden retrievers, and border collies are just a sampling of the breeds used in search and rescue work. Dog handlers that belong to the American Rescue Dog Association, however, prefer German shepherds as their partners.

German shepherds have physical characteristics that make them fine choices for search and rescue. The breed's sensitive nose is well known for its keen scenting ability. In addition, a double coat of fur helps keep the dog warm in cold weather conditions and protects it in the heat.

A German shepherd's medium size makes it easy for the dog to fit in the confined spaces of pick-up trucks or helicopters on the way to a rescue site. In addition, they are muscular and agile, and they can work long hours over difficult terrain.

Caroline Hebard, co-leader of Northeast Search and Rescue, was handler to Aly, an American Rescue Dog Association certified German shepherd. At 9:00 p.m. one autumn night, Hebard received a call for help. Twelve children had gone for a walk in the wilderness near the Delaware Water Gap in Pennsylvania. They had left in the afternoon and hadn't returned.

When Hebard and Aly arrived at the search area, the temperature was a frigid 10°F. The children had to be found quickly, or they would easily die from the cold. The team immediately began their search. Aly used tracking and air scenting to follow the children's scent. Within a few hours, Aly brought Hebard to a boy's footprint and pursued the scent with renewed excitement. Soon after, Aly raced around a bend and returned to Hebard with a stick in his mouth. That meant he had located the children.

The kids were fine, but they were very cold. They cuddled with their hero dog for warmth as they sipped warm fluids. Aly's excellent search skills saved the children's lives.

investigate the booming sound. Displaying this type of confidence and curiosity is an important trait for wilderness search and rescue dogs. The dogs shouldn't cower behind a tree when they hear the jarring sound of a helicopter whirring overhead or the various noises of an active search and rescue site.

Next, Gallagher places the puppy on its back on the floor and holds the pup in that position for a few moments. During this test, Gallagher looks for a puppy that will struggle for a bit but then relax. A puppy that acts this way shows he has independence, but will also allow the handler to train him. After choosing a puppy that seems suited for wilderness search and rescue, the job of training the canine to become a masterful wilderness search and rescue dog lies ahead.

Training for the Wilderness

When the right pup has been chosen, its handler begins to teach the dog the necessary skills for succeeding in wilderness search and rescue work. A handler usually begins the training by exposing the puppy to various experiences and people in order to allow the dog to become comfortable in many situations. This process is known as **socializing**.

An important part of socializing is having the puppy become comfortable with people. A search site is filled with different groups of people, such

Handlers make sure their dogs become familiar with walking on rock, tree roots, and other surfaces.

as police officers and rescue volunteers. Search and rescue dogs need to stay calm and focused amid the bustling activity. No one wants a search and rescue dog that will bite rescue personnel or the person the dog finds. The socialization process starts at the handler's home, where the puppy might learn to accept young children squealing and romping around. The pup also gets used to various noises, such as the doorbell ringing or people talking. These experiences ready the learning pup for rescue sites.

Search and rescue dogs often have to walk over rough terrain, such as tree roots and rocks. The puppy needs to become accustomed to different materials under its paws, so a handler exposes the puppy to various textures underfoot, such as kitchen floor tiles, backyard grass, and driveway asphalt.

Many times, search and rescue dogs have to travel in vehicles for long distances before reaching the search area. To prepare a pup for this, its handler may take the dog on frequent car trips. This allows the canine to become used to settling quickly and lying patiently until it is called to duty. Gallagher had an imaginative way to help Lektor practice these skills. She asked a theatre owner if she could bring Lektor into the establishment while she watched a movie. Using this technique, Lektor learned to settle at Gallagher's feet for hours.

Obedience training is also an important part of search and rescue training. Imagine that a dog and its handler are involved in a wilderness search. The dog becomes so focused on scenting that it bounds toward a cliff. The handler must be able to command the dog to stop before it falls over the drop. Obedience training helps search and rescue dogs learn to listen and respond quickly to their handlers' commands.

Another part of training that Gallagher finds useful is participation in Schutzhund. The sport helps keep Lektor's obedience and scenting skills sharp. Schutzhund also tests a dog's protection abilities by using various personality-testing techniques. In one exercise, a person plays the role of bad guy and wears a bite sleeve on his arm. This padded sleeve protects the volunteer from a dog's bite. During training, Lektor learns to bite the sleeve when Gallagher gives him the correct command.

Not all search and rescue dog handlers include protection work in training. Some handlers question the necessity of teaching a dog to bite when the job doesn't require it. Other search and rescue specialists, like Gallagher, believe that protection training teaches the dog control. At one point in protection trials, Lektor is told to approach the person with the bite sleeve and just bark, known as the bark and hold. At other times, he is commanded to bite the sleeve, and Gallagher orders him to immediately release it. Exercises like these require extreme obedience and

WATER SEARCH AND RESCUE DOGS

Once a dog has been trained to find a person by following human scent through the air, the canine can be taught to participate in water search and rescue. Many wilderness and disaster dogs are cross-trained in water searches.

Most water search and rescue work is actually the search for and recovery of drowned individuals. The dog and handler are transported by boat across the water where it is believed that a person has drowned. The dog is able to detect the person's scent in the air after it rises through the water. The canine might alert its handler to strong human scent by digging at the bottom of the boat or by barking. Then, divers will be sent into the water to search for and recover the person's body.

Training for this work involves the same hide and seek games that most search and rescue dog handlers use during training. But in water search and rescue, the training helper is outfitted with a diver's air tank in order to hide deep in the water. The dog

(continues)

Water search and rescue dogs are trained to air scent in order to find the location of a drowned victim.

(continued)

is commanded to locate the helper and alerts to his scent. If the task is completed correctly, the dog is quickly rewarded with a toy and plenty of playtime.

In water search and rescue, handlers need to understand how air and water currents affect scent. They also need to take water temperature into consideration when directing their dogs—human scent is generally stronger in warm water than in cold water.

Amazingly, water search and rescue dogs have been known to find drowned bodies under as much as 100 feet (30.5 m) of water. By locating a drowned person, these dogs and their handlers offer peace of mind to the victim's family members.

control for the dog. Gallagher believes that a dog that has learned to respond with control is less likely to bite a person unexpectedly.

FOLLOW YOUR NOSE

Most search and rescue dogs learn air scenting to locate a lost individual. In addition to air scenting, Lektor is cross-trained in tracking, a search tactic the dog uses to follow a human scent or footprints on the ground.

To teach Lektor to track, Gallagher initially walked a straight 100-foot-long (30.48 m) track. She placed small bits of hotdog in the toe of each of her footprints and one of Lektor's toys at the end of the track. She wanted Lektor to learn that when he completed a track, someone would play with him.

Over time, the tracks became longer, more challenging, and filled with twists and turns. In addition, the tracks were laid through more challenging terrain, such as in thorny shrubs or in wooded areas. And the hotdog hints were stopped, too; a person lost in the wilderness would not be dropping tasty treats in her footprints!

After Lektor mastered tracking, he and Gallagher tackled air scenting. To start this training, Gallagher enlisted the help of a family member who took Lektor's toy and ran away while the dog watched. When the helper hid from Lektor's view, Gallagher would command her dog to "go find." Lektor would locate the helper, who would play enthusiastically with the canine. As air scenting training progressed, Sherri covered Lektor's eyes so he wouldn't see where the helper ran and hid. This way, Lektor learned to rely on his scenting ability to find the hidden person. Because search and rescue dogs almost always have to find people they don't know, Gallagher eventually replaced her family-member helper with a friend, and finally, with a stranger.

With all of this training, the search and rescue dog gains the experience it needs to track and find people who desperately need help.

On the Trail with Bloodhounds

A confused, elderly man had suddenly wandered away from his home. He had been missing for 2-and-a-half days when Deputy Terry Davis, of the Loudoun County Sheriff's Office and president of the Virginia Bloodhound Search and Rescue, received a call to help. Davis and his female bloodhound, Belle, responded.

Davis knew Belle would be the right fit for the job of finding the lost man because she had done the same work before. He brought Belle to the lost

Deputy Terry Davis can read his bloodhound's behavior. When Belle is hot on a scent trail, her tail sticks up and her body becomes tense.

man's house and placed her in her harness, which had a long tracking lead. Then Davis gave Belle the man's bed sheets to sniff. The sheets served as scent articles, which are items such as bed sheets or clothing that contain an individual's unique scent. The man's skin rafts and bacteria left on the sheets would aid Belle in her search.

When Deputy Davis gave Belle the "track" command, the bloodhound was off and trailing the lost man's scent. Twenty-six minutes later, Belle and Davis located the man in a ditch. The dog and handler team had saved the man's life!

Bloodhounds like Belle have the skill to gather a particular scent and trail a specific person. This breed was originally bred to hunt game animals, but in the 16th century, landowners used bloodhounds to trail people who were stealing animals from their property. Today, bloodhounds continue to be known for their special ability to trail people.

Bloodhounds trail scent rather than track it. This dog breed finds the most recent scent and pursues it. Bloodhounds don't follow a person's footsteps, as tracking dogs do. How do these searching types differ? Picture this: a person enters a baseball field near the dugout, runs the bases, and leaves through a different exit near home plate. The tracking dog would work around all the bases and then exit just as the man did. A bloodhound, on the other hand, would enter the park and head directly to the place the man exited.

Because bloodhounds trail only one person's scent, they are not distracted by the scents of other people who might cross the trail and contaminate it. For this reason, explains Davis, a bloodhound's specialty is searching places with many people, like suburbs and cities.

A bloodhound has the skill to gather a particular individual's scent and trail it to that specific person.

PARTNERING UP

When Davis was looking for a pup, he visited a blood-hound breeder to observe the litter of bloodhound pups. He looked for a puppy that would approach him to play because Davis needed a friendly pup that was not aggressive. His future bloodhound also had to display independence and confidence, so Davis paid attention to pups that walked off to investigate their surroundings. Working bloodhounds must be comfortable taking the lead on a trail. After evaluating these qualities, Davis saw that one particular female puppy would be the right choice for him.

After Deputy Davis chose Belle, he took her to many different places to begin her socialization. She tagged along to the sheriff's office and even visited highway truck stops with her handler. Belle needed to become used to various places and people, and Davis didn't want her to become nervous about new experiences. As a search and rescue canine, Belle would have to stay calm in all environments and with many rescue personnel around her.

Davis did not focus on obedience training with Belle because a bloodhound needs to act independently on the trail and not look back toward the handler for commands. Instead, Davis and Belle worked on training.

To help with Belle's training, Davis enlisted a friend. The training volunteer dropped a scent article, such as his hat, to the ground. Then, he took one of Belle's favorite food treats, ran 10 to 20 feet (3.05-6.1 m) away, and hid. Deputy Davis had Belle sniff the scent article and then he commanded her to "track." When she found his friend, she was awarded with food. Bloodhounds love to eat, so food is used to motivate and reward them.

During the second phase of trail training, Belle watched the friend run away and hide. Now, though,

MADE FOR SCENT WORK

Bloodhounds are physically designed for following scent trails. A bloodhound's nose is structured in a way that helps the dog be especially good at smelling. The dog has 220 million olfactory receptors, which help it gather scent. In addition, its nostrils have extra-long slits that make it easier to inhale odors. A bloodhound's brain aids its nose with scent work because a large portion of the dog's brain is devoted to the sense of smell.

A bloodhound has deep folds in its face that hold scent close to its nose. The slobbery jowls keeps scent moist and active. Also, the dog's long ears drag, stirring up skin rafts that have settled.

Handlers can assist the dog's natural ability to scent. Terry Davis, president of the Virginia Bloodhound Search and Rescue, makes sure that his bloodhound, Belle, has enough water to drink. This keeps her nose moist and better able to detect smell. Blood-hounds make wonderful use of their unique physical traits to trail individuals. These dogs are especially known for working trails that are days old. Nick Carter, a bloodhound handled by Captain the friend continued to move farther away while Belle couldn't see him. This way, she was forced to use her sense of smell to find the hidden person. Davis also taught Belle to jump onto the person she locates.

Gradually, the scent trails became more challenging as they increase in distance and turns. The trails eventually ran through deep brush and thick woods. Belle was taught to follow trails that been laid hours

Volney G. Mulliken of Lexington, Kentucky, was able to follow a trail that was 105 hours old—that means it was laid almost four-and-a-half days before the dog was brought on the scene.

Bloodhounds are especially known for working trails that are days old, making these dogs well-suited for missing person searches.

or even days before her arrival. This helps sharpen a bloodhound's unique ability to follow old trails.

To help Belle succeed with trail work, Deputy Davis had to understand how scent travels on air currents. He knows that moisture could keep a scent alive and smelling strong. On the other hand, hot, dry conditions can bake skin rafts, so there is little or no scent for bloodhounds to pursue. This knowledge helps Davis when he and Belle are called to duty.

Davis and Belle have trained so thoroughly together, that he can read the canine's behavior. Davis knows, for example, that when Belle is hot on a scent trail, her tail shoots up and her body becomes tense and filled with purpose.

One time, Belle and Deputy Davis were asked to trail a criminal who had broken into a car and tried unsuccessfully to steal it. Davis placed a sterile gauze pad on the driver's side headrest, where the criminal had sat. He left the pad in place for 5 to 10 minutes, and it absorbed some of the man's rafts. Then, he put the gauze in a plastic bag to use as a scent article for Belle. Deputy Davis and Belle trailed the criminal and played a vital part in his capture.

Disaster Dogs

A massive earthquake hits in a distant country, collapsing tall buildings and homes. Thousands of people are buried in massive piles of rubble that are filled with jagged debris. The U.S. State Department requests the help of the Federal Emergency Management Agency's (FEMA) Virginia Task Force One. Virginia Task Force One is one of only two FEMA groups sent to disaster areas overseas. Elizabeth Kreitler, a canine search specialist with Virginia Task

Force One, awaits a call to duty with her male German shepherd, Nero.

Nero is a highly trained urban search and rescue canine that's certified by FEMA. He and Kreitler might be called to find people buried in rubble following a natural disaster, like an earthquake, hurricane, or tornado. They also search when the disaster is human-made, such as an airplane crash or a train derailment. The team works wherever they are needed, whether in the United States or abroad.

When Kreitler's pager beeps to alert her that she and Nero are requested for an international mission, they drive to Dover Air Force Base in Delaware. There, 62 VA Task Force One members and, at most, six disaster dogs board an Air Force C-5 Galaxy, one of the largest airplanes in the world, for their important trip.

In addition to transporting the human and dog members of the Task Force, the C-5 is loaded with must-have supplies to support the mission. Large tents to house the workers, as well as food and medical supplies for both humans and dogs are among the many items needed. In all, 60,000 pounds (27,215 kg) of equipment, including small trucks and an 18-wheel tractor-trailer, are loaded onto the airplane. Additional supplies are brought specifically for the dogs. Collapsible water bowls for hydration, kiddy pools for bathing and decontaminating them after their workday on the debris pile, and hairdryers for drying their fur are vital pieces of equipment for the dog team.

Often times, air travel on the military plane can be difficult for Nero and his fellow canines. It could mean the dogs have to travel in crates for up to 24 hours with no way to go to the bathroom and with little food or water. Once the team lands in the country of their destination, they still might face hours of travel by bus, train, or boat to reach the disaster

Disaster dogs respond to human-made disasters or natural disasters such as this one, a mudslide in California.

site. Still, these dogs don't let these situations stand in the way of doing what they do best: searching for survivors or victims.

In the case of an earthquake, Nero and Kreitler begin searching as soon as they arrive at the disaster site. Most live victims are recovered in the first few days following an earthquake, so it's critical that the team quickly begins work. Normally, the canine teams work 12-hour shifts, but during life-threatening times, they might work 24 hours—or even longer—at a stretch.

Search and rescue dogs like Nero are never really off duty at a disaster site. Even after the grueling hours on the rubble pile are over, Nero helps cheer up the community. Children, who may have lost family members or their homes, approach Nero to pet him. They often tell Kreitler stories about their own dogs and talk about their lives before the disaster. "It is rewarding to bring joy to a disaster site," Kreitler says.

FINDING THE RIGHT DOG

Like other handlers who look for certain qualities in their search and rescue dogs, Kreitler knows what she needs in a puppy. First, she starts at a respected breeder and looks for a puppy that loves to play. Toys and playtime with their human handlers are used extensively as rewards in disaster dog training.

Kreitler also wants a confident puppy because a canine with a meek personality would not make a successful disaster dog. Disaster search and rescue canines are often asked to lead the way onto a dangerous rubble pile. If the handler cannot navigate a section of the debris, the canine will need to venture

RESCUE IN MEXICO

An earthquake hit Mexico City on September 19, 1985. The earthquake was a powerful magnitude 8.1 on the Richter scale. A team of disaster dogs and their handlers were flown from the United States to help. Caroline Hebard and her German shepherd Aly were part of the important team.

An 11-story clothing factory in a poor section of the city had collapsed with the workers still inside. Nearly a week had passed since the devastating earthquake. The crumbled structure was ready to be bulldozed, but the relatives of the workers believed they heard sounds of life beneath the rubble. They begged authorities to delay the clean-up process. They asked for aid to help find any survivors.

The U.S. canine search and rescue team raced to search the factory. Soon, Aly alerted to live human scent. Two women were alive under the rubble! How had the victims survived while being trapped for almost a week? A window near their heads was broken. When it rained, the drops fell through the opening in the window, and the women were able to catch the water in their mouths.

Caroline Hebard and Aly, along with the other search and rescue team members, had saved the survivors' lives!

into the area alone. Dogs training for this type of work must have the confidence and ability to work independently.

When she has found her pup, Kreitler starts to expose the dog to all kinds of people and other animals, including dogs. Disaster sites are bustling with strangers, like firefighters and construction specialists, and other searching canines. The dog cannot be aggressive with other people or animals, and it shouldn't be distracted by them either.

An urban search and rescue dog, especially one that works on international missions, must be accustomed to long periods of travel. To prepare Nero for this part of the job, Kreitler brought the puppy on frequent car trips. When Kreitler has the opportunity to fly on a plane, she brings Nero along for the ride—and the experience.

With his socialization well underway, Kreitler turns her attention to Nero's formal disaster dog training.

Preparing for the Worst

An urban search and rescue dog, like Nero, has to be agile enough to walk on chunks of concrete and crawl through small spaces in the rubble. Kreitler trained Nero to be sure-footed by exposing him to different tests of agility. As part of this training, Kreitler encouraged Nero to jump straight up and down like a cat does. Jumping in this manner keeps the rubble beneath him from moving too much.

Nero also practiced crossing a wooden beam high above the ground and crawling through narrow tunnels. He walked across a seesaw, which taught the dog to wait until it balanced before he could continue walking. This skill comes into play when material on the rubble pile shifts underneath the dog's paws.

CALLED TO KATRINA

On August 29, 2005, Hurricane Katrina barreled into the coastal areas of Mississippi, Louisiana, and Alabama. The storm brought ferocious winds of 145 mph (235 km/h). Some locations were hit by a 30-foot (10 m) storm surge, which is a wall of water higher than the rooftops of most houses. Homes were destroyed and more than 1,000 people were killed by the effects of the hurricane.

Federal Emergency Management Agency's Virginia Task Force One was asked to help search for people. Elizabeth Kreitler and her urban search and rescue dog, Nero, were among the teams to respond. They were sent to Gulfport and Biloxi, Mississippi.

Nero and Kreitler searched all types of collapsed structures, such as one-family houses and apartment buildings. Some of the houses were still standing, but the storm surge had piled the home's furnishings so high that Kreitler couldn't enter the buildings. That's where Nero's search and rescue canine ability came into play. Nero could climb easily over chairs and coffee tables to search for survivors.

Sadly, Nero discovered one person who did not survive the hurricane. Even though the hope is always to find live victims, Nero and Kreitler have given the person's family peace of mind. The individual's loved ones have answers about what happened to the person and have a body to lay to rest.

Climbing a ladder is a must-have skill for disaster dogs, which sometimes need to reach the top of a rubble pile or to board a plane that's heading to a disaster site.

Disaster dogs sometimes are required to climb ladders, for example, to board airplanes or head to the very top of a rubble pile. Kreitler trained Nero to work on a ladder with flat rungs that was positioned parallel to the ground. She placed a piece of dog kibble on each rung to coax him across. When Nero became comfortable with where to place his feet, his handler raised the ladder to a 45-degree angle. Eventually, Nero learned to climb a ladder with round rungs.

Disaster dog handlers need to be able to tell their dogs which way to go on the debris pile. Kreitler practiced directional commands with Nero on an area shaped like a baseball diamond. She stood on home plate and sent him from base to base using the commands "left" and "right." She also told Nero to "go out," which means to move away from the handler, and "go back," which means to move even farther away.

At each base, Kreitler placed a raised, large wooden platform. When Nero arrived at the base, she would verbally command "hup" and use hand signals to match the command. Kreitler paired her verbal commands with hand signals to prepare Nero for searching at noisy disaster sites, where it can be difficult to hear the handler's voice. Kreitler's directions told Nero to jump onto the object, which is an essential skill for search and rescue dogs to have when locating a lost individual.

Disaster dogs are trained to lie down and be still when in a harness or secured to a moving platform, like this rescue dog at the World Trade Center site.

Kreitler taught Nero to air scent using the same hide-and-seek techniques used by wilderness canine search and rescue handlers. An urban search and rescue dog, however, does not perform the find/refind alert that a wilderness dog does. It would be far too dangerous for the disaster canine to cross back over the unstable rubble to warn his handler in this fashion. Instead, disaster dogs learn to give a 30-second bark alert.

Kreitler taught Nero the bark alert by making the dog bark to receive his toy. Later, she introduced the

WHO'S ON THE CREW

Search and rescue dogs were not the only canines to help after hurricane Katrina. HOPE Animal-Assisted Crisis Response sent therapy dogs and their handlers to Baton Rouge and New Orleans, Louisiana. The canines visited with victims of the hurricane at disaster centers and temporary housing areas. Many of these people had lost their homes, possessions, and some had even lost family members. Petting and hugging the dogs lifted the victims' spirits and reduced their stress. The dog teams also helped disaster responders feel better after their difficult days of work.

HOPE dogs need to be prepared to work near disaster sites. The dogs learn to accept all sorts of unusual noises, such as sirens and alarms. Since the dogs are often exposed to crying people, and receive bear hugs, and kisses on the muzzle, they have to be bark barrel, which is constructed of two 55-gallon (208 liter) drums that are securely joined together. The barrel is equipped with a plywood door, which has small holes drilled in it to allow human scent to escape. The holes are placed at the bottom of the door to teach the dogs to search low for scent because most disaster victims are buried under debris.

At first, a training helper took Nero's toy and crawled into the barrel. She did not cover the barrel with the door. Nero found her, barked, and the person played with him. As training progressed, the helper

comfortable with this. Before the dogs and handlers go to work, they complete a three-day workshop for certification. Many breeds of dogs can participate in this type of work, including bichon frises, Boston terriers, and mixed breeds.

Jill Cucaz, HOPE's Eastern U.S. regional director, and her golden retriever, Custer, were among the teams that responded following Katrina. Cucaz remembers the teams visiting with local families who had lost their homes and had been living on Carnival Cruise ships for more than three months. The children smiled and laughed as they stroked the dogs and took them for short walks around the ship. Their moms snapped photographs of the kids having fun with the dogs. Those pictures of happy times would replace photographs that had been destroyed by the hurricane.

covered more and more of the barrel's opening with the door, until she hid in the barrel with the door completely closed. Finally, Nero would be brought to the area after the helper entered the bark barrel. In this way, he learned to locate an inaccessible person and give a loud, long bark to alert his handler.

In more advanced training, firefighters on the Task Force helped Kreitler and Nero practice rappelling. The firefighters placed the human and her dog in harnesses. Kreitler held Nero between her legs, and the firefighters lowered them from a four-story practice bay to the ground below. This experience prepares the team for a situation in which they must be lowered by ropes down the side of a building. It also helped Nero remain calm when suspended, just in case he ever fell through the rubble and needed to be raised by a harness and ropes.

Having undergone such intense training, Nero and Kreitler can be counted upon to respond valiantly to any disaster. They are ready to board the C-5 whenever the pager sounds.

7 Avalanche Dogs

An avalanche of snow rushes down a mountain like a river, swallowing large trees and burying everything in its path—even people. A fast moving avalanche can travel up to 120 miles per hour (193 km/hr) and cause a freefall of tons of snow. The avalanche might be a powder avalanche, consisting of loose snow, or a slab avalanche with enormous chunks of packed snow and ice.

The cause of an avalanche, called the avalanche trigger, can be naturally occurring. During a storm,

Patti Burnett and her avalanche search and rescue dog, Hasty, spend some downtime in the snow. Hasty assisted in numerous heroic avalanche search missions.

the added weight of heavy new-fallen snow on already existing snow might trigger an avalanche. A blustery wind could blow additional snow onto snow layers that cannot support the extra weight, starting an avalanche.

The trigger can also be human-made, such as a skier or snowmobile rider who ventures outside of designated safety areas, adding weight to unstable backcountry snow. Human-made triggers also include ski patrols and officials who set off mini avalanches to

prevent large ones from occurring naturally and putting people in serious danger. Controlled snow slides
like these are well-planned and highly organized so
that no people are injured.

Avalanche search and rescue dogs are specially
trained to use their keen sense of smell to locate victims who were in the path of an avalanche. Hasty, a
male golden retriever, was an avalanche search and
rescue dog that was known for his excellent ability to
find avalanche victims. Hasty and his handler, Patti
Burnett, worked with Copper Mountain Ski Patrol
and Summit County Search and Rescue in Colorado.
The handler and dog team were always ready to
respond to an avalanche call.

On January 7, 1994, an avalanche hit in Summit
County, Colorado. Burnett was out checking trails
for safety when the radio call for help sounded: an
avalanche had buried a person.

Luckily, another handler who had trained with
Hasty was able to rush the dog by snowmobile to the
avalanche site. Hasty began digging at a spot in the
snow, a skill avalanche search and rescue dogs use
to alert that they have located a strong human scent.
Soon after, Burnett arrived and continued to work
with her dog.

Rescuers poked long poles, called probes, into the
snow where Hasty had alerted. They touched a person with the probes and discovered a young woman,

Avalanche search and rescue pups, like Magic, need to display energy, endurance, and persistence. Handlers like Patti Burnett know these are key traits for their dogs.

buried under 3 feet (.91 m) of snow. She had been buried for about 14 minutes and had a weak pulse. Luckily, medical experts on the scene were able to revive her. After one night in the hospital, the woman returned home to her husband and children.

"Finally all those hours and years of sore shoulder muscles, wet gloves, and cold feet had paid off. She was alive!" Burnett said. "I still wonder whether Hasty fully recognized how thrilled I was with his magic nose."

That was just one of Hasty's heroic search and rescue missions. But sadly, Hasty died on April 10, 2000. Today, Sandy and Magic, Burnett's other golden retrievers, continue Hasty's important lifesaving avalanche search and rescue work.

PUPPY PERFORMANCE

Handlers who want a talented canine, like Hasty, begin by carefully choosing the correct breed of dog. For avalanche work, the dog breed must be known for its superior scenting ability and warm coat of fur that will help protect the dog as it searches in frigid temperatures.

Sometimes avalanche search and rescue dogs have to be transported to an avalanche site by ski or snowmobile. Here, Sandy poses with Patti Burnett and a friend.

Most avalanche dog handlers choose medium-sized breeds, like Labrador and golden retrievers or German shepherds. Even though larger breeds could do the work, they present some challenges. It can be tricky to transport a 150 lb. (68.04 kg) Newfoundland to an avalanche site by chairlift or in the small confines of a helicopter.

THE SAVIORS OF TRAVELERS

If you were the victim of an avalanche in the 19th century while trekking through the Swiss Alps from Italy to Switzerland, a St. Bernard might have helped you. The monks of St. Bernard hospice used the dogs to rescue lost travelers and victims of avalanches in the Great St. Bernard Pass, which is 8,000 feet (2,438 m) above sea level.

The St. Bernards worked in groups to help avalanche victims. The dogs would use their keen sense of smell to locate a person buried in the snow. Then, the dogs would dig through the snow until they reached the victim. If the individual was unable to walk, one of the dogs cuddled close to him to provide warmth, while another raced to the monks for help.

One of the monks' St. Bernard dogs, Barry, has been credited with finding and saving the lives of 40 people in the early 1800s. All told, the dogs of St. Bernard hospice were saviors to over 2,000 travelers.

Today, helicopters and modern search equipment have replaced the St. Bernards' rescue work, but their legacy as heroes of the Alps remains.

Search dogs have to be accustomed to the sounds and scents on an avalanche site, such as a whirring helicopter and other handlers and their dogs.

After deciding on a breed, handlers turn to breeders of reliable working dogs to purchase their puppies. Handlers have many important qualities that they look for to indicate which pups might be successful avalanche dogs.

John Reller is an avalanche dog handler with the Copper Mountain Ski Patrol and the Summit County Search and Rescue in Colorado. When he picks a puppy, like his female golden retriever Tracker, he looks for an independent pup. At an avalanche site, the dog must be confident enough to venture out quite a distance from the handler in search of human scent. Reller looks for a confident dog that will continue to follow its nose no matter what the challenge.

Avalanche search and rescue pups also need to display lots of energy. Working avalanche dogs might need to trek for miles to and from an avalanche scene. They also search for hours at a time and return day after day until a victim is located. These dogs need to have endurance and persistence.

Dean Cardinale, forecaster for safety at Snowbird Ski and Summer Resort and the president of the Wasatch Backcountry Rescue in Utah, is the handler of an avalanche dog named Midas. When Midas was a puppy, Cardinale put the German shepherd through a series of tests to evaluate the dog's potential for avalanche search and rescue work. Cardinale threw a toy to see if Midas would chase it and bring it

Dean Cardinale put Midas through a series of tests to evaluate the dog's avalanche search potential. Today, the two are part of the Wasatch Back Country Rescue in Utah.

back. He wanted a puppy with a strong drive to play because avalanche dogs are rewarded with a toy and a rousing game of tug of war during training.

As part of the puppy evaluation, a handler might pop an umbrella open near the puppy. He would like to see a pup that won't be frightened by noise because sometimes an avalanche dog must ride on a loud helicopter to reach the site or must search through howling snowstorm winds to locate a victim. Dogs chosen for this work aren't afraid of sounds.

To socialize Midas, Cardinale brought the dog to schoolyards filled with children. He even took the canine on swimming trips. These social activities helped Midas become comfortable with all sorts of people and various situations.

Avalanche dogs also must become accustomed to the various types of travel to and from avalanche sites. Handlers take their pups-in-training for rides on chairlifts, snowmobiles, and helicopters. The dogs have to accept the feel of skiing, as well. Reller, for example, wears Tracker around his neck like a scarf as he skis to the avalanche area. Reller doesn't let Tracker walk to the site because he wants his dog to save her energy for the search.

Training Heroes of the Snow

Avalanche dogs and their handlers train often and vigorously to sharpen their search and rescue skills. The dogs learn to detect human scent as it travels in the air and how to follow the scent to discover a victim buried deep in the snow.

Once the pups have been socialized, it is time to begin formal avalanche dog training. At an avalanche site, search and rescue dogs work off the lead, which is a long leash, so the handler needs to be able to control the dog's behavior from a distance. Cardinale taught Midas to respond to commands such as "come," sit," and "stay." Midas also learned to move left or right when his handler commanded him with hand signals.

The scent of a person buried in an avalanche rises through the snow to the air above. To teach the dogs this air scenting skill, handlers might play a fun game of hide and seek on the snowy mountains. When John Reller taught Tracker to air scent, he enlisted a helper who would hold Tracker while Reller ran away to flop into the snow and hide. The helper released Tracker, who raced to her handler for an enthusiastic game of tug of war with her favorite toy, a glove.

During each step of air scent training, Tracker would seek out the helper, who also hid because the dog needed to learn to look for a person other than her handler. To further challenge Tracker, Reller covered her eyes before the person ran away to hide. This forced the dog to rely on her nose, rather than her eyesight, for searching.

For the next portion of training, Reller dug a trench in the snow. When he ran away, he jumped into the snow trench. This way, Tracker understood that she was looking for someone beneath the snow's surface. Then, he dug a few trenches in a row and hid in one. Tracker had to use her sharp sense of smell to discover which trench held her handler.

Avalanche dogs alert handlers by digging when they find a victim. To teach Tracker to dig, an assistant shoveled snow onto a helper who was in the trench. When Tracker located the hidden individual, Reller dropped to his knees, dug in the snow, and encouraged the dog to do the same. Some days, Tracker practiced with experienced avalanche dogs, which showed her how the digging should be done.

Avalanche dogs are taught to dig near a buried person's face in order to expose the victim to oxygen as quickly as possible. To train for this, the buried helper tucks the dog's reward glove into the neck of his jacket. Why? In a true avalanche situation, the person's scent is stronger near the face because it is the only part of the body not covered with clothing. In addition, the person's breathing gives off scent that is detected by the dog.

During advanced avalanche dog training, a person is buried deep in a snow cave. To build the cave, a large hole is made in the snow. A cave—big enough for a person to fit comfortably while lying down—is dug at the bottom of the hole. A volunteer enters the cave and blocks of snow are used to close up the entrance. The hole to the surface is filled with loose snow. Volunteers don't need to worry about being buried though. The cave has enough air for three hours of breathing time.

Avalanche dogs and their handlers train vigorously to keep their skills sharp. This dog is entering a snow cave during a practice training session.

Dog trainers allow 10 minutes to pass, which lets the helper's scent rise from the cave to the air above. Then, the dog is commanded to search until the canine locates the person and gives a dig alert.

SHARPENING SEARCH SKILLS

Avalanche dog handlers like to challenge their canines during training. John Reller creates scenarios for Tracker to find more than one buried person. This helps Tracker learn to search for multiple victims because an avalanche sometimes strikes an entire group of skiers.

On the other hand, some avalanches aren't witnessed by anyone, which causes rescuers to worry that a person might be trapped under the snow. For this reason, Tracker also trains where nobody is buried. This allows Reller to read her behavior when an avalanche site has no victims. This training helps

John Reller and Tracker ride on a ski lift on their way to an avalanche training area. Reller has learned to read his dog's cues to determine if any people were buried in an avalanche.

Reller and the search teams safely rule out the possibility of buried people.

To further challenge Tracker's skills, Reller sometimes sprinkles tasty dog treats around the search area. This teaches Tracker to work hard, no matter how tempting the distractions.

Patti Burnett uses similar techniques to train Sandy and Magic, but she introduces gasoline fumes to the dogs' training. Why the fumes? Snowmobiling is a popular sport that, when done in backcountry areas, can trigger massive avalanches. When an avalanche hits a snowmobile, the machine often overturns and gasoline spills from the tank. The overpowering fumes from the gasoline make it tricky for the dogs to detect human scent. By introducing these strong fumes to Sandy's and Magic's training sessions, Burnett hopes the dogs will become accustomed to tracing a human scent, despite competing, strong odors and fumes.

Dean Cardinale has entire cars buried in the snow for Midas's training. Sometimes, avalanches slide over highways and swallow cars in the process. This type of training exercise allows Midas to work on his search and rescue skills in situations similar to what could be found on a real avalanche site.

In addition, many avalanche search and rescue dogs are taught to locate personal items, such as hats, gloves, or backpacks buried in the snow. These items hold a person's scent because they were in contact with the person. Searching for these articles can be a challenge because they only contain a small amount of scent. But if the dog uncovers an article at an avalanche scene, the item might provide important clues. The article could alert rescuers that a person was definitely caught in an avalanche. Perhaps the victim was swept farther than the object he lost, or the item traveled beyond the victim's final location. In either case, the buried individual will probably be found in

Handlers like to challenge their avalanche dogs to locate people in difficult situations. This trainer helps his canine dig through a snow trench during practice training.

a direct path uphill or downhill from the location of the object.

HANDLER KNOW-HOW

Avalanche dog handlers must be knowledgeable in order to help their dogs successfully search snowy sites. Handlers need to understand how wind speed and direction affect the way human scent moves in the air. The handlers also must know the different

AVALANCHE SMARTS

Handlers and their avalanche rescue dogs have seen first-hand the death and devastation an avalanche can bring. For this reason, they emphasize the importance of avalanche preparedness and safety awareness.

Staying within the safety of a ski resort is the safest route to take when it comes to avalanches. But people venturing into the back-country for skiing, snowboarding, or even hiking should check with local ski patrols for avalanche reports. It's a good idea to ski with friends, and everyone in the group should carry avalanche safety equipment. Skiers should ski one at a time, while the others in the party watch closely. This way, only one person at a time is exposed to risk. This method also allows other members of the group to identify the area where the person was last seen if avalanche occurs. Then, they can begin searching for the person immediately and perhaps save his life.

types of avalanches and how they allow scent to escape to the air above the snow. A powder avalanche, for example, can fill every nook and cranny around a buried person, so his scent takes longer to reach the surface. A slab avalanche has pockets of air around the blocks of snow, so scent can rise more quickly. However, handlers must also be aware that the scent might travel around chunks of snow, only to be released far away from the victim's location.

What should you do if you are ever caught in an avalanche? Dean Cardinale recommends that you try to ski downhill and to the outer edge of the avalanche in an attempt to escape it. Patti Burnett suggests dropping anything that might weigh you down, such as a backpack. She advises trying to grab hold of trees or rocks to stop yourself from being swept down with the wall of snow.

John Reller suggests that you thrust an arm or leg toward the snow's surface, which could help rescuers locate you. Moving your limbs out and pushing snow away from your face might also provide an air pocket to supply some oxygen. But tumbling in an avalanche can be disorienting. To determine which way is up, drool or spit. It will always travel downwards with gravity. Watch the drool and thrust your arm or leg in the opposite direction. This could create an air pocket or even show rescuers your location.

Unfortunately, no matter how well-trained the search and rescue team, most avalanche missions don't recover living victims. The best period to make a live find is within 15 minutes of the slide. By the time a call for help is received and the dogs and handlers reach the area, the opportunity for live rescue has often passed.

The best chance for a person to be found alive after an avalanche is to be discovered by members of his skiing party. When venturing into the backcountry, skiers should always travel with buddies. Each skier should wear a transceiver inside his jacket and should have a collapsible probe and shovel in his backpack. This way, a skiing group will have the tools they need to possibly find and free a buried friend.

Heroic dogs, such as avalanche search and rescue dogs and disaster dogs, play an important role in helping to save human lives. Because of the hard work of these canines and their dedicated handlers, people who are victims of nearly every type of emergency can depend on highly-trained canines to assist in the rescue efforts.

Glossary

air scenting A dog's ability to smell and follow a human's dead skin cells as they float in the air

agility The ability to move quickly and with grace

avalanche A large mass of snow, ice, rocks, dirt or other material in sudden movement down a mountain or other slope

rafts Dead skin cells that float on air currents and have a particular odor that a canine can detect and follow

Schutzhund A dog sport that includes tracking, obedience, and protection work

socialization Exposing a dog to different social settings

temperament Mental or emotional traits

Bibliography

American Rescue Dog Association. *Search and Rescue Dog: Training the K-9 Hero.* New York: Wiley Publishing, Inc., 2002.

Burnett, Patti. *Avalanche! Hasty Search.* Phoenix, Arizona: Doral Publishing, 2003.

Burnett, Patti (Copper Mountain Ski Patrol and Summit County Search and Rescue; Avalanche Search and Rescue Dog Handler). E-mail interview with the author, October 12, 2005.

Cardinale, Dean (Snowbird Ski and Summer Resort, Forecaster for Safety; Wasatch Backcountry Rescue, President; Avalanche Search and Rescue Dog Trainer and Handler). Telephone interviews with the author, October 12, 2005; October 17, 2005; October 18, 2005.

Corns, Bryan (New York State Police, Trooper; Bloodhound Handler). Interview with the author, Rhinebeck, New York, August 27, 2005.

Davis, Terry. "Scent Collection and Preservation." *Eastern Armed Robbery Conference Gazette.* February 2001. http://www.earc.org/v4n149/Information5.shtml

Davis, Terry (Virginia Bloodhound Search and Rescue, President; Bloodhound Trainer and Handler). Telephone interview with the author, September 29, 2005.

Dobnik, Verena. "Dog Used in Search of Attack Site." Associated Press. September 24, 2001. www.firehouse.com/terrorist/24_APdogs.html

Flood, Mary (Federal Emergency Management Agency Utah Task Force One; Urban Search and Rescue Canine Search Specialist). Telephone interview with the author, February 18, 2005.

Gallagher, Sherri (Chicago Regional Search and Rescue, President, Training Director, and Search and Rescue Dog Handler). Telephone interview with the author, September 19, 2005.

Jackson, Donna M. *Hero Dogs: Courageous Canines in Action.* New York: Megan Tingley Books, 2003.

Kreitler, Elizabeth (Federal Emergency Management Agency Virginia Task Force One; Urban Search and Rescue Canine Search Specialist). Telephone interviews with the author, July 14, 2005 and October 13, 2005.

McDaniel, Melissa. *Disaster Search Dogs.* New York: Bearport Publishing Company, Inc., 2005.

Merritt, Carl (Dutchess County Sheriff's Department, Deputy; Bloodhound Handler). Interview with the author, Poughkeepsie, New York, February 3, 2005.

"Monks Seek Homes for St. Bernard Rescue Dogs." Reuters. http://msnbc.msn.com/id/6197922

"Profile of a Rescue." Federal Emergency Management Agency. www.fema.gov/usr/about2.shtm

Reller, John (Copper Mountain Ski Patrol and Summit County Search and Rescue; Avalanche Search and Rescue Dog Handler). Telephone interview with the author, October 18, 2005.

Serlin, Mitch (Westchester County Police Department, Police Officer; Bloodhound Handler). Interview with the author, Poughkeepsie, New York, February 3, 2005.

Syrotuck, William G. *Scent and the Scenting Dog.* Mechanicsburg, PA: Barkleigh Productions, Inc., 1972, 2000.

Whittmore, Hank and Caroline Hebard. *So That Others May Live.* New York: Bantam, 1995.

For More Information

Find out more about the training and work of the dogs in this book by contacting these organizations.

American Rescue Dog Association
P.O. Box 151
Chester, New York 10918
www.ardainc.org

Federal Emergency Management Agency
500 C Street, SW
Washington, DC 20472
202-566-1600
www.fema.gov

National Association for Search and Rescue
703-222-6277
www.nasar.org/nasar/
info@nasar.org

National Police Bloodhound Association
www.npba.com

Search and Rescue Dogs of Colorado
P.O. Box 1036
Fort Collins, Colorado 80522
www.sardoc.org

Summit County Search and Rescue Group

www.scrg.org

Virginia Bloodhound Search and Rescue

www.vbsar.org
vbsar@shentel.net

Wasatch Backcountry Rescue

Dean Cardinale
WBR P.O. Box 920133
Snowbird, Utah 84092
wasatchbackcountryrescue.org

Further Reading

Gorrell, Gena K. *Working Like a Dog.* Toronto, Ontario: Tundra, 2003.

Greenberg, Dan. *Wilderness Search Dogs.* New York: Bearport Publishing Company, Inc., 2005.

Jackson, Donna M. *Hero Dogs: Courageous Canines in Action.* New York: Megan Tingley Books, 2003.

McDaniel, Melissa. *Disaster Search Dogs.* New York: Bearport Publishing Company, Inc., 2005.

Presnall, Judith Janda. *Rescue Dogs.* San Diego, CA: Kidhaven Press, 2003.

Silverman, Maida. *Snow Search Dogs.* New York: Bearport Publishing Company, Inc., 2005.

Wilcox, Charlotte. *The Bloodhound Vol. 2.* Mankato, MN: Capstone Press, 2001.

Web Sites

American Kennel Club
www.akc.org/breeds/index.cfm?nav_area=breeds
Pictures and descriptions of various dog breeds.

Dog Owner's Guide Online Magazine
www.canismajor.com/dog/sandresc.html#Intro
Information about search and rescue dog training and work.

Federal Bureau of Investigation
www.fbi.gov/kids/dogs/search.htm
Learn about the FBI's search and rescue dogs.

Federal Emergency Management Agency
www.fema.gov/kids
Find out about FEMA
www.fema.gov/kids/games/heroes
Pictures and trading cards of FEMA urban search and rescue canines.

National Geographic
www.nationalgeographic.com/ngkids/0301/index.html
Facts about avalanches and avalanche safety.

Working Dog Foundation
www.workingdog.org/kidskorner.html
Provides information about working dogs and helpful links.

Picture Credits

Index